No Matter What,
The Past Cannot Change

No Matter What,
The Past Cannot Change

M.A. Howard

J. Kenkade
PUBLISHING®
Little Rock, Arkansas

No Matter What, The Past Cannot Change
Copyright © 2020 M.A. Howard

Printed in the United States of America

J. Kenkade Publishing
6104 Forbing Rd
Little Rock, AR 72209
www.jkenkadepublishing.com
Facebook.com/jkenkadepublishing

J. Kenkade Publishing is a registered trademark.

Printed in the United States of America
ISBN 978-1-944486-52-5

Table of Contents

Part One   9

Part Two   19

Part Three   27

About the Author   39

About J. Kenkade Publishing   41

Five things you will never recover in life...

A stone after it's thrown
A word after it's said
An occasion after it's missed
Time after it's gone
Trust after it's lost

Part One

Everybody has a story; this is mine.

Before I was born, this is the story I was told was about our family history from my grandma, who I knew as "Mama." Mama's daddy had a cotton farm in the 1900-1920s, around 500 acres, which was pretty good for farmers. When he died, his kids got 120 acres each. This was good income for their families. There seemed to be tragedy and sadness before I was even born. Mama's daddy had a still (moonshine), and one day the sheriff came by. Mama said he had to talk to her daddy about something. She just knew he was there to take her daddy away to jail. She said she was scared to death. But he didn't go to jail and time went on.

They worked the fields. Maw, Mama's mother, cooked and took care of the home. She was a stern woman, no nonsense. She was of Choctaw nation from Oklahoma. Mama said her daddy found Maw and brought her back here to Arkansas, where they had 3 daughters and 2 sons. Mama's brother Ronnie died in the Army in Texas of a heart attack on his 21st birthday. She said the funeral home driver drove in snow all the way there and all the way back. That is all I know of that part of life.

I guess Mama met Joe sometime after Ronnie died. Joe was my grandpa, my mom's daddy. I don't know a whole lot about him. Just what Mama would tell me. He was mean to her. He would get drunk, be gone with his brothers, and spend all his money. She was a meat cutter and wrapper at Kroger. That was good considering she was a 3rd grade drop out. She also had to help with her family and work the farm. She hated the sun. She had lots of freckles and being in the sun would make them worse. Mama also had a very bad stutter. She said she broke her own self of that habit. I think our whole family down the line had bad habits, and somehow we just kept going.

In January 1948 my mom (biological mother) was born, a cold month. I don't know a whole lot through these years, except what I was told by my aunts and uncles and Mama. I believe every word Mama told me. Because of her raising me early on is why I turned out the way I did. She did show me and tell me the truth. She taught me to be good to others, to be grateful and thankful. Every day I am. So, here is what I was told by Mama. My mom met Tim and they got married. Her mom and daddy, my grandparents, built her a house when she got married. Her cousins told me how she got the record player and all the 45 records. They said they were lucky they got $50 when they got married, but Mom never let that cross her lips to us.

She talked about how bad everyone was to her, and that was not true, so I guess it was always in my mom to be hateful. Family says how they didn't want to be around her. Cousins said she acted like she was too busy to be around them. My mom, when she was older, was a very pretty woman, but she used people. Family talked about how hateful she was. Nobody wanted her around. Even as a child, they said she was no good, and I don't mean that lightly. There are people that are just no good, and I believe she was one of them. I don't like saying that because she was my mom, and I did love her.

She got married to Tim, then came Tommy, their firstborn son. Then came Corey, not long after Tommy. Mama said Tim would burn Tommy with cigarettes. I don't know what all really went on during this time, I wasn't even born yet. But if it's anything like the way things were after me, there was a problem going on inside my mom's head even then because I have to think it was a sickness that made her have no love in her heart and her soul. How can your own mom hate you just because you were born, like me? Or hate one so much, just because of who their father was?

I need to back up a minute. You see, when they were building my mom and Tim a house, it was behind Mama's little convenience store she had, while Joe drove his concrete truck. She said they were doing very well back in that time, but it was the start of a cycle that went on. And someday to stop. You see, Mama was a functional drunk. She said she would have her PBR under the counter (Pabst Blue Ribbon). She said Mom would call her "a no-good drunk." Mama said how she would cry. She felt so lost and alone. She said they lived in Michigan for a while; that's when she was working at Kroger. I guess it was walking distance from their house because she said she came home one day and Joe had another woman in the house. He locked her out, while he had someone else in her home. How do you think that is normal of any sort? Or how you tell someone that is what you're supposed to do? You were not born to be mistreated by another human being, and Mama was, by her husband and her only child, her daughter.

I was born February 6, 1963. My mom said she hated me from the time she found out she was pregnant with me. She told me she was in a phone booth making an appointment to have an abortion but passed out. And from all my heart, I would have given anything for her love, but it just was not there. You've got to have love in your heart to give it. In 1964, my mom tried to commit suicide. She laid me in front of the gas stove, and she took an overdose of sleeping pills. The babysitter got worried when she didn't bring me that morning, so she came to see what was wrong and found us and called the police. Where Tommy and Corey were at that time, I don't really know. I was told that Tommy and Corey were put in an orphanage, I do not know why. I never found out. So, after the attempted suicide, they put my mom away in some type of mental institution. I do not know how long she was in there. I know the family went to see her. What happened that year is anybody's guess. I went to live with Mama then, and she raised me for a while.

Sometime around 1965, my mom married Stan, Tim's brother. She had a baby boy named Cajun, and she hated him because of who his father was. Joe, Mom's daddy, died that year. He got his paycheck, and I guess he and his brothers got together drinking and riding in the back of a, what we called, a turnip truck. Mama's sister told her he was getting some when he supposedly fell out of the back of the truck. Why didn't they look for him? Go back. Instead they left him. Did he die instantly? Did he live a while? No one will ever know that except his brothers. When they found him, his body was in a ditch, bloated and no money on him whatsoever. Mama said she believed his brothers rolled him, not meaning to kill him. That's why they didn't say too much about it, but I think Mama believed they had something to do with it. Just the fact that they didn't go back to look for him. Who knows, they may have seen he was already dead and took his money and left him, as to not get themselves in trouble and be questioned about the incident. I can just imagine how Mama felt. Honestly, I don't think she was too upset because of the way he treated her. I think he ruined her. She was 45 and never married again. Maybe it was meant to be? Only God knows our plans, and I believe it was meant for her to be there for me, even if it was for a little while. Maybe it was a time I needed to be shown what love was, and I mean a love like no other, unconditional love. Because it was not waiting on the road. My mom was at the funeral home after they did the autopsy and lifted the top off his head and looked inside and said, "I knew the son-of-a-bitch didn't have any brains," and she walked out.

In 1966, I guess life was calm during this period. I can remember sitting on Paw's lap, going through the cotton fields, stopping and getting a drink of cold water coming out of the pipes that were watering the fields. Paw and Maw, my great-grandparents, would watch me walk through the cotton fields to my aunt and uncle's house. That was a time nobody locked their doors. They would leave the windows open to have that night breeze. The innocence of times and ourselves. Even as I write this, the memories are coming back. Sounds crazy, but I've even had a smell come pass me that I haven't smelled since I was little, like Mama was here for just a moment. In 1967, I was 4 years old. I can remember spending the night with Paw and Maw. I was kind of a sickly child, stomach problems. Paw would be up with me. Maw would be asleep in her recliner. Life was good. I don't remember my mom too much. She was in California mostly. Mama and I would go see her sometimes. We would take a bus, sometimes we took planes. They would come see us, too. I just don't remember seeing them that often.

Then the day came. Maw came running and hollering for Mama. All I know is that Mama pushed me back into the house. All I remember is Mama and Maw screaming and crying, running towards Maw's house. Well, I was determined to go too, to see what was going on. All I remember is running behind them. I ran in the house, right behind them. I don't know if I saw his head, but I remember the blood going under the dryer. How thick and dark red it looked, still running, moving slow. I don't remember anything else about that. My Paw was gone; he had shot himself. As life went on, we had long summer days sitting on the back porch, snapping beans, shelling purple hull peas. I would look at Mama, and she always had a smile on her face. I guess that's why I always had one on my face. Love knows love.

In 1968, Mom tried to commit suicide again. She was put away again in the institution. She must have been in there awhile. Mama and I would drive up to see her. She made me a navy and yellow dress. I still did not know who she was to me. Sometime around 1969-1970 I was hanging upside down in a Mimosa tree one day. Maw came up to me and asked why I called Mama, "mama." I just looked at her and said, "Well, she's my mama." And that was it. I asked Mama about it later in years, and that's when she said Maw wanted her to tell me she wasn't my mama, but she didn't want to at the time. I still don't remember seeing my mom much.

Part Two

In 1971, when I was 8 ½ years old, Mom and Ed, her third husband, wanted me to come live with them. I was so happy to have a mom and dad. Well, we moved into a trailer park in Memphis for a little while. It was funny because Mom said we were going towards this big beautiful house and how pretty it was, but turned out to be this run down trailer. Then, we moved back to Arkansas into a very little tiny house, but it was by the city pool. That was great. Mama got me swimming lessons. I loved swimming. Things were ok. Mom didn't care much for me. She never smiled. It was like she hated the world, but it was just me and Cajun that made her so miserable. She hated who we were. We were her mistakes.

Then the darkness came. When my new daddy came into my room, not to tuck me in and give me a kiss on the cheek and tell me goodnight. NO! My world turned upside down in a matter of minutes. I did not invite him to my room. He came in and helped himself to me. He asked how I liked it. I was not a woman. I was a little girl that wanted her new daddy to love her. Everything I believed in, went out the door. He didn't use his penis. It was just his hands, but it was every night. I never slept again. To this day, I'm still scared of the dark, and I trust no one. I was always so tired at school. I was so sleep deprived. I put some Chester drawers against the door. He would push it open.

During the day I stayed at the swimming pool and at night, when it was open. This pretty much went on for 4 years. By now I was used to it. It was a regular thing. I just can't believe that no one saw or heard anything for all that time. 4 Years of not being able to say something to someone. I couldn't hardly stand it at times. His breath, his smell. He smelled so bad. He didn't take baths regularly, and to get up the next day like nothing happened. Well it did happen, and it will affect you in ways you never thought. And for someone to say, "Oh, get over it." Until you have been where I have been, do not judge me. How do you go on and not go totally insane? My nerves were shot at 10 years old. How does someone so young make it through that? You learn you have no friends you can talk to. They're just not real. The thing was, I knew who the boogeyman was, who was coming into my room. Still the same, I hated the dark. If you come to my house now, there are nightlights everywhere.

In 1972, everything was pretty much the same. Ed would take me to the gas station where he worked, and when it wasn't busy, he would come in the back and mess with me. Ed never let up on me. I just learned to survive. Mama moved to town to be closer to us. I wanted to go back with her so bad. She thought it would be best if I stayed with Mom. She just had no idea what was going on. On February 5th, 1973, Maw shot herself in the head just like Paw, the day before my 10th birthday. My uncle had that gun destroyed after that. It would never be used again. Now why did she choose the day before my birthday? I have no answer to that. One of Mama's sisters stopped talking to her. She blamed Mama for moving to town and thought that's why Maw did it. Mama was so hurt, not only by losing her mother, but to get blamed for it also. Poor Mama.

In 1974, I was 11 years old. My half-brother and two of his friends raped me. They blind folded me, but I peeked and saw who they were. One's a millionaire in Texas. Life goes on. Ed is still coming into my room, and I guess I got tired of it. In 1975, I was 12 years old. I went to the bedroom where mom was sleeping. She was asleep on one of the twin beds. I walked and slid down the wall between the beds and told her I needed to tell her something. I started crying, and I told her what Ed had been doing. OH my god! What did I just do? She jumped up out of bed. Now, this is someone who does not care anything about me. So, she grabs me by the hair, pulls me down the hallway to the living room, where Ed was watching GunSmoke, and she asks him, "Have you been fingering my daughter?" At first, he said no. When he did that, I looked him dead in the eyes and told him, "Yes, you have been doing it for years." Then he said he had been. So, she stays with him, and she starts looking for a husband for me in the paper. I'm 12 years old. I'm being punished for something I had no control over. I did not ask for that.

Mom found Chad. I was 12 and he was 19. She picked him out for me, and he had no idea what he was in for. He worked at the gas station that Ed did. Just a kid. Chad made me feel like someone cared, like he was going to be my protector. He was gonna save me. You see Chad never knew. Nobody knew. My uncle told me if he knew what was going on, he would have killed Ed, and said, "I'm sorry, but I would have killed your mother, too." My aunt said he was not lying either. Me and Chad were the talk of the town. People talked about our ages, me from the dysfunctional family, and his family was about to explode. Chad's daddy was going back to his first love, and they are still together today.

How wonderful of a team Chad and I were. We dated, and my mom pushed for marriage right off the bat. "Get married, get married!" She had to get me a husband. Now remember, I'm only 12 years old. Life seemed a little safe for the moment. We went to the movies, hung out, and rode around in his car. We talked about life together, getting married, and having babies. He loved me. That was all I wanted. We became sexual, and did not use birth control; I'll put it that way. I was 12 years old, and my mom wanted me to do all this so she would look like she had an out of control daughter, and then people would feel sorry for her. She's the whole reason this is happening. Poor Connie. How I hated her so much, but I never disrespected her or talked back to her. I loved her. I was a good girl, and she made me look like a bad girl. This was someone you never said no to. You see, people don't understand. A paranoid schizophrenic is a very disturbed person. When she gets mad, over nothing, she starts throwing things: coffee cups, lamps. Seriously! People wouldn't believe she was that way because she was good, very good, at showing a different side that the outside world didn't see. Sometimes I thought I was living with the devil himself because she was such an awful person. To me she was.

Let's get on with Chad and me. Like I said, we were the talk of the town. We were just kids. In December 1975, the Vietnam War ended, Jimmy Hoffa disappeared, Jaws, the movie came out, Bruce Springsteen's "Born to Run" song came out. Me and Chad ran off together. It was just after Christmas, and he came and picked me up. We already decided we were running away. We were getting out of there. I got in his 2-door Ford, slid over there next to him, put that blue eyeshadow on, the kind he liked. We were on our way. Don't know where, but somewhere. We made it to Oklahoma. Money didn't go far. We learned that very fast. We stayed there a few days, then money ran out. We had enough to get back home. Well, we started home, not realizing the police had been looking for us. Pretty sure Chad's mom called the police because this was exactly what my mom wanted. Sympathy, having a daughter to put you through something like this. She could turn the tears on as fast as she could turn them off. Split second change. Like my aunt said one time, "I never talked back because she probably would have killed me." If they only knew.

When we made it back, the police were over us. Next thing I knew, we were in a courtroom. I was on the stand. The judge asked me questions, why I ran away. I never said a word. I sat there and looked at my mom and Ed and thought, this is because of you. I didn't stand up and say what was going on in that house of nightmares. You can say, well you weren't too scared of her to do things I did, but you don't understand. This is what she wanted. The drama. "Oh me. Poor me!" So, Chad and me, we couldn't talk or see each other. No phone calls, no in person contact at all. How was I gonna survive without him? I believe whatever happened with us, was to save me for a minute. Keep my sanity. This was the first time I tried to commit suicide. I took my mom's valium. I didn't take enough, and I got very sick. Never told her what I did, but I think she knew.

Part Three

In 1976, at 12 years old, I found out I was pregnant. My mom made an appointment for me to have an abortion. She had it scheduled for February 6, 1976, my 13th birthday. We were in the office about to have the abortion, and I'm crying. I didn't want it. She looked at me with such hate and said that if I didn't have it, my clothes would be in a cardboard box sitting by the road, and I would be there with them. So, I had the abortion. We got home, I'm bleeding so bad and was weak. I thought I was bleeding to death. I was so sick; I had a high fever. She brings me a chocolate cake and puts it down on the coffee table and wishes me a happy birthday. I thought I would be dead by morning, but I wasn't.

Things are a little fuzzy at this point. Life went on, but me and Chad weren't gonna be kept apart. During the court deal, they gave him an option, go to jail or to the service. He went into the Navy. Time goes on. We're writing letters and calling each other. Mom knew all this. That's how she worked it. The first time he came home on leave and got home, he called me. Next thing I knew, my probation officer was at my door. He said they knew I was talking to him because his phone was busy at the same time mine was. Well, we got together again anyway. Now his mom knew all this, too. She came to pick me up and take me to the airport to pick him up when he came home on leave. She took us and his sisters to the lake. We were so young. Me, I had only one thing on my mind, to get the heck out of my house. This is just the tip of the stories that won't get written.

Chad comes home on leave in July. We go swimming and to the movies. Just hanging out, me and him. I was so young, and I knew I loved him, but I knew he loved me. It might have worked if it was later in years. I don't know. Well, I found out I was pregnant again in August. This time I was keeping it. In a way, that was music to my mom's ears. She saw the money then. We got married at the courthouse in the small town we lived in. Oh my gosh! I bet the town was buzzing. Now that I'm older and look back, I can just see my mama now. We were together for 10 days, basically. He left and went back to the Navy, and again, I went into survival mode.

Because she and Ed would fight all the time, I was always the main character in their fights. I was her daughter during the fights. Then, I was a "sorry whore, no good, never wanted you, nobody will ever want someone like you, all used up trash that you are." You know you hear that almost all your life, and you do start thinking that she has to be right, I am no good. I always said I was damaged goods. I can be glued back, but I will always have a crack that nobody sees. Because of you, I can't and will never be complete. To go through the horrors, and they were horrors to me, the trust you once had is gone. I'm 57, and I still have a hard time trusting. I hate to use the word horror in this because I know someone has had it worse than me. And I can only imagine, because I know. I SURVIVED.

So in between time, I pretty much tried to stay out of everybody's way. I did what I was told. Life went on. I tried to go to school, but I was ridiculed. When I was standing in the lunch line, this guy stepped out of the lunch line and yelled at me, calling me a f------ whore. I just slowly turned and walked away. I went home and told Mama I was never going back to school again, and I didn't. I got a GED when I was 16. I learned the rest from life lessons. Here's a few things that happened in between. I was 13, married and pregnant, living in a mobile home with just the lights on. Chad had to trade his motorcycle and car in as a down payment on the mobile home. If my mom didn't want me in the house, she would have me stay in the trailer with a little heater as the only warmth I had.

She hit me in the stomach one time. I was about 5 or 6 months pregnant. We went to the K-Mart cafeteria to get lunch, something she never did. All I got was some mashed potatoes and gravy. Next thing I knew, I was on the floor with potatoes all over me. My mom leaned down and told me not to move. Then she starts acting all concerned over me, so they helped me to the truck. Nothing was wrong with me. My mom told me to stay in the truck, and she went back to the store. When she came out, she had an 1800-dollar check. Go figure. That is how she rolled. She would shoplift; be cool about it, get to the check out, she opens her purse like nothing is in it. I knew what was in it. She was at my mama's house and was telling Mama that she shoplifted in California but not here in Arkansas. I looked at her and said, "Yes you have, you had me stand in front of the cart while you filled your purse up." She got so mad, she jumped up and left. She lived across the street.

When I was 13, I met Tim, Tommy and Corey's daddy. I thought he was mine too, but that's when I found out, I was not who I thought I was. He told me my mom was in Chicago when he and her daddy, Joe, went to get her. He said she was already pregnant with me when they picked her up. I have never met my father to this day and still don't know who he is. It is what it is. So, Tim told me pretty bluntly, "I'm not your daddy." There it was again. The Trust. My god, who do you trust? Who do you believe? Family? Friends? Almost all of them have lied to me. So, I try to be honest, to be good, and it is hard when your family is the way mine is. Sometimes I did want to give up. I tried suicide again at one point and failed.

I'm gonna back up a second. During my early childhood years, it could have been good at times.

We would go get what we called "free cheese." Commondies, best cheese in the world. We went to the State Fair in an old farm truck. I remember thinking that I was gonna roll out of the back going up and down that hilly road, but I didn't; I'm still here. Mama and I would go to California and visit mom. We would go to the ocean. Mama always had a cloth diaper on her head. We would go to the big flea market. Tommy and Corey would put me inside a Goodwill box. We found all kinds of stuff. I found a long blonde wig once; Mama threw it away soon as I got home. It was fun to run around, pick grapes, and eat them. We rode dirt bikes in the desert. I slept in the garage with them, and one night there was a mountain lion at the door. That's when I had enough of sleeping out there. I stayed with Mama after that. One time Mama and I took a plane out to California, they served us some meatballs, and my mama took a bite. She hummed that they tasted so good. I took a bite, and as soon as I did, she started laughing. She said, "Oh honey, spit that out!" It was so bad tasting. Later in the year, I saw some of the same meatballs and asked what they were. They were called Swedish meatballs, and I said I would never eat them again. Just talking about them brings back the memories. When I was 10 years old, she took me down to Fish Hatchery road, what we called an old gravel and dirt road. That's where I learned how to drive. That's where she took my kids, her great grandchildren, and let them learn.

In April 1977, I had my baby girl. I had 3 pains, and they gave me what they called twilight. When I woke up, I had a baby. I loved that baby more than life itself. She was the one thing I could love, and she was mine. It's hard to understand unless you have been there to know that feeling I'm talking about. Even at the hospital my mom made Mama cry from making fun of her in some way, just hateful. Other than my mama, my daughter had all my love that was in me. And trust me, I had the love, just nobody wanted it. So, I'm 14 with a baby, my mom is no better. Life goes on. Mom and Ed would fight all the time. Once they were fighting so bad, she kept saying how "you finger my daughter." She put him down like a dog. He took it. He knew she would have him put in jail, so he put up with her ranting all the time. They were fighting so bad one night, he had a 357 Magnum at her head, she had her head hanging off the bed in a room that was added on. I was so sick of hearing her say that. I said, "Shoot her, just shoot her" under my breath. I'm so sorry I said that, but it never stopped, her bringing me up every time they had a fight. She stayed with him. I accepted that. He was never really mean to me after that, but I hated her more than I did him. It sounds crazy. It was because she wouldn't let it go. Remember, I learned at an early age that I didn't matter. I didn't matter.

In June 1977 at 14 years old, I lied about my age because I looked older and got my first job at this restaurant in town. Pretty sure he knew I was underage. Anyway, I bought the diapers and formula. Chad sent money, too. Now that I'm older, I really hate how things happened so many years ago. He was good, just not the right time. People say how we looked alike, and his birthday was the day after mine. It's sad. We got divorced, and I don't remember a whole lot during that time, except his mother was bent on taking me to court every time I turned around. That was diaper money, formula money, and clothes money. Chad didn't pay a lot, but in the beginning he paid the price for meeting my mother on that fateful day he met her. I pretty much worked and took care of my baby. I didn't date; nobody wanted to date me. The in-laws left me alone for a while.

In 1978, I was 15 years old. This was a year, I guess, that was as normal as it was supposed to be. I tried suicide for the last time that year. Mom and Ed still fought, I worked and didn't have any friends. I had one friend growing up. Annmarie was her name, and she lived next door to us. Then one day she was gone. She went to live with her grandma. Later in the years, I saw her and we talked. She said her stepdad was messing with her. I told her about Ed, and she said she knew he was messing with me. How, I didn't know. I wonder sometimes now, was my neighborhood a place of predators? Because Mom, Ed, and the neighbors got together and played cards. Were all the women on valium. Ed had a Boa snake for a pet, and they would talk about that and so on, but these men would want me to make them a sandwich or bring them cigarettes and beer. When I would bring it or serve them, whichever sounds best, they would try to pat my bottom and thank me, or rub my leg and arm like you shouldn't be doing to a young girl. So, I often wonder, was it something they talked about?

In 1979, when I was 16 years old, I was working at Stuckey's gas station. Then that one ex in-law wanted to start trying to get my daughter again. Here we go again, me spending money I didn't have on a lawyer to fight to keep her. I met Toby, and we dated. My mom started pushing marriage, not me, but between mom and the ex in laws, I was going nuts. I thought marriage would get everyone off my back. We were married for 3 months. We weren't mad at each other; he would tell people it was my crazy mom. So, my mom moves the trailer I lived in out to the country on some land she bought. One day she got a call that the field caught fire and burned the trailer some, but not all the way, so that night she takes me out there and drops me off. She drives on down the road. I knew what I was doing was so wrong, but you didn't say no to her. Well the trailer was too wet to finish burning it down, thank God. When I got older, I would think about it. To think she drove off so if I got caught I would be the one in trouble for the fire, not her. She was smooth. My mama was always in the picture. Mom was always mean to her, and she did nothing but help her and all her kids. I saw Mama crying over how Mom would treat her. She would always tell me to just overlook her. I guess that's what everybody did, overlooked her meanness, sickness, forgive her. That is something I've got to do is forgive her. Pray at the end of my story I will. Well life goes on. It wasn't a simple one. I was on nerve pills by then, and the family doctor would tell me I worried over things I couldn't do anything about.

In 1980, when I was around 17 years old, I got a job at Maybelline. Life went on. I worked and took care of the baby. My half-brother, Corey, was getting married out of state. He wanted Mom to come, but she wouldn't, so he had me to come. Why? He had no use for me. Anyway, a girl at work was gonna take me to the airport and keep my 1968 VW, and then come pick me up when I got back. That's when I met Neil, the father of my second daughter. His sister said he was head over heels for me. When I got back to work from the wedding, I saw Neil maybe 2 times. Then one night when I came home from work, my mom was sitting in the kitchen in the dark smoking a cigarette. My clothes were thrown out in the hallway. I asked her what was wrong. She said there was evil in that room and whatever it was wanted me out. She threw me out that morning with no warning and no place to go. I couldn't go to Mama's, Mom would just make her miserable, so Tommy's, my half-brother who raped me with friends, was the only place I had to go. I stayed there a week, then moved in with Neil, only because I had no place to go. Life was ok. Then another story comes along. And no, love did not come softly.

When you read this, you will say, how can that happen? It did, and I'm like so many others. We have similar stories, but there is not one the same. We were made to be ashamed, never talk about what went on, made to pretend like we were a normal family. I didn't know what was normal. I thought I was normal, then as I got older, I knew there was something horrible in that home. What I have talked about is just a portion of what life was like living in a dysfunctional family, so when I see families, kids, moms, dads, I wonder. I can't help it. What goes on behind closed doors? My pieces are glued back together, but if you look close enough you will see the cracks of my life. When you go through something like this, you never get over it. You never forget, but you do go on. I'm proof. I will always be broken, not by choice, but I have come to terms with that. I want to enjoy my life. I'm 57 and just now found my voice, and I won't hold back no more. I FINALLY FOUND HER...ME! This is my story.

By M.A. Howard

M.A. HOWARD was raised in a small country town. She is a loving wife, mother, grandmother, and great-grandmother. She enjoys cooking, shopping, and spending time with her family. M.A. loves to write and has some stories to tell! She looks forward to sharing her stories and helping others who have been through a lot in life. Her passion and desire is to help others feel understood and not judged or ashamed for what they've lived through. She was lost at one time, but not anymore. She says, "I finally found her… Me!"

Our Motto
"Transforming Life Stories"

Publish Your Book With Us

Our All-Inclusive Self-Publishing Packages
100% Royalties
Professional Proofreading & Editing
Interior Design & Cover Design
Self-Publishing Tutorial & More

For Manuscript Submission or other inquiries:
www.jkenkadepublishing.com
(501) 482-JKEN

Also Available from
J. Kenkade Publishing

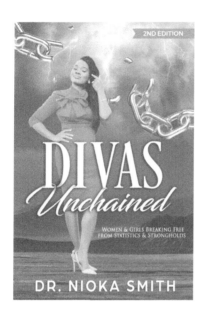

ISBN: 978-1-944486-25-9
Visit www.drniokasmith.com
Author: Dr. Nioka Smith

Sexually abused by her father at the age of 14, pregnant at the age of 17, and a nervous breakdown at the age of 28, Dr. Nioka Smith's painful past almost killed her, until the voice of the Lord guided her into destroying strongholds and reversing Satan's plan for her life. DIVAS Unchained is the powerful chain-breaking reality of the many unfortunate strongholds our women and girls face. Dr. Nioka uses her divine gift to help women and girls break free from destructive life cycles and prosper in all areas of life. Satan has lied to you. It's time to expose his lies. It's time to break free!

Also Available from
J. Kenkade Publishing

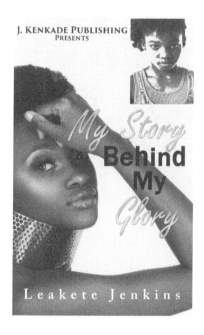

ISBN: 978-1-944486-14-3
Visit www.jkenkadepublishing.com
Author: Leakete Jenkins

The story of a young girl born with medical issues and throughout her childhood, suffered molestation, tried to commit suicide, was involved in an abusive relationship, and felt as if no one cared for her. This book will invite you into a story that is so heart-breaking, but will also show you that through any obstacle, God will see you through.

Also Available from
J. Kenkade Publishing

ISBN: 978-1-944486-23-5
Visit www.jkenkadepublishing.com
Author: Vanessa Farr

Black Eyes and a Pure Heart is a novel about the life of a young girl who must figure out how to live her life with a child at the age of 17. When the baby is born, her supportive spouse becomes an abusive predator. The black eyes represent the malicious nature of the domestic violence in the face of evil that so desperately tried to kill her. This short story reveals that the wrong path in life can gravely disfigure and blacken the eyes of young women and girls who seek easy pleasure.

Also Available from
J. Kenkade Publishing

ISBN: 978-1-944486-37-2
Visit www.jkenkadepublishing.com
Author: Yolanda Turner Evans

Based on a real life story (the story of Yolanda Turner Evans) that made nationwide headline news. Yvette Diaz was violated and raped at the early age of nine by several family members. Feeling alone and unworthy as a teenager, she starts to look for love in all the wrong places. She has trudged through a long journey of hurt and pain and is the product of a deceased mother and absent father. She finally grows tired of running to survive and settling to keep the peace. She realizes that she's not a problem, but a solution to a world that was dying from the exact same thing she had experienced as a child.

This page intentionally left blank.

J. Kenkade Publishing

Made in United States
Cleveland, OH
24 March 2025